It Happened to

ME
Drug Addict

Interviews by Suzie Hayman and Helen Elliott

W
FRANKLIN WATTS
LONDON•SYDNEY

© 2002 Franklin Watts

First published in Great Britain by
Franklin Watts
96 Leonard Street
London
EC2A 4XD

Franklin Watts Australia
56 O'Riordan Street
Alexandria
NSW 2015

ISBN: 0 7496 4335 8
Dewey Classification 362.29
A CIP record for this book is available from the British Library.

Printed in Malaysia

Interview on pages 12-19 by Helen Elliott, all other interviews by
Suzie Hayman

Series editor: Sarah Peutrill
Art director: Jonathan Hair
Design: Steve Prosser
All photographs David Montford apart from Colin
Edwards/Photofusion: 22 posed by model. Matt Hammill: 12, 14.
Crispin Hughes/Photofusion: 42 posed by model.
Idalina/PYMCA: 32. James Lange/PYMCA: 18. Julia
Martin/Photofusion: 4b, 38. Pav Modelski/PYMCA: 36.
Naki/PYMCA: 33. Stuart Saunders/Photofusion: 35 posed by
model. Ian Simpson/Photofusion: 9. Bob Watkins/Photofusion: 17.
Gavin Watson/PYMCA: 4t, 30.

Consultants: Helen Brookes and Phil Mythen (Health Promotion
England)

With grateful thanks to our interviewees and Holly Lodge
Secondary Unit, Lancashire.

Contents

Introduction

What are drugs?
A drug is any substance that changes the way you think or feel when you take it. Every society has drugs of some sort. People smoke tobacco, dried mushrooms, cannabis or heroin. They chew leaves or drink distilled fruit or grain (alcohol).

Drugs and the law
In most countries, alcohol, caffeine and tobacco are legal drugs. Some drugs, such as tranquillisers, are also legally available through a doctor on prescription. There are laws against misuse of some of these drugs. So, it's not against the law for someone under 16 to have or use cigarettes or alcohol. But a shopkeeper would be breaking the law by selling these to children.

The UK Misuse of Drugs Act makes it illegal to have, sell or give, grow or make certain drugs. These drugs are divided into three categories. Class A drugs are the most dangerous. These include cocaine, crack, ecstasy and heroin. Class B drugs include speed, barbiturates

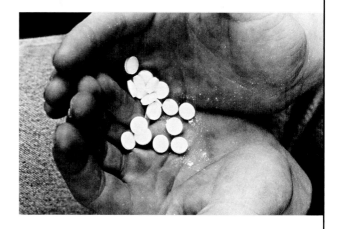

(downers) and some tranquillisers. Class C drugs include minor tranquillisers. The penalties for having, selling or giving them depend on the class of drug.

How will this book help me?
Drugs are widely available these days, whether you live in a big town or a small village. You might be offered drugs, you'll hear about them and you'll almost certainly be curious. So what are the facts and what do you think about them?
It Happened to Me - Drug Addict lets you see the issue from the viewpoint of people who have been there and done it. They don't preach and they don't tell you what to do or what to think, but their stories may help you sort out your own ideas on the subject. Before you make a decision to try anything, it's worth knowing as much as you can about drugs and drugtaking.

Note on the interviews
The interviews are written as closely as possible from the words of the interviewee. They are written in Question and Answer format (Q and A). Alongside them you'll see some interesting facts and figures and talking points, which should help you to start thinking about some of the more complex issues.

If you're worried about a friend or relative who is taking drugs:

◆ Try to talk to them about it.
◆ Find out how drug-taking is affecting them; how are they handling it?
◆ Educate yourself about drugs and encourage them to do the same.

If you're thinking about trying drugs:

◆ Ask yourself why you want to try drugs. Is it curiosity or peer pressure? Are there deeper problems in your life which you want to escape?
◆ Read the stories in this book. What can you learn from them?
◆ Be as informed as you can. Contact the agencies or look at the websites listed on page 46 for further information.

If you are a drug taker:

◆ Take a moment to examine your life. How is drug-taking affecting your personality, work and relationships?
◆ Be as responsible as you can. Every time you take something be aware of how your body feels before and after. Don't take drugs on your own, make sure you have someone you trust with you.
◆ If you want to slow down or stop taking drugs and need help, speak to your doctor, a close friend, or contact one of the agencies listed on page 46.

It Happened to Sanita

Sanita is now 19. She was 12 when she first smoked cannabis. By the age of 16 she was using crack cocaine and smoking heroin, but she never injected drugs. She was studying for a law degree but today she is in a treatment centre, learning to live without drugs. She hopes eventually to go back to studying and become a solicitor.

Q When did you start using?

A I started using cannabis at the age of 12. By the time I was 13, I was using crack and at 16 I started smoking heroin. I wouldn't inject, I was more into drug smoking. I didn't really like alcohol.

Q How did you get on with your family then?

A Me and my family didn't really get on. When I was two my dad gave me to his brother. When I came home I was rejected, I wasn't a part of their family. I was always the outcast of the family.

Q Did you start using because of your family life?

A Before I started using, my life was full of pain and hurt. I couldn't deal with that. I had to find another way of dealing with it - by using drugs. It took that pain and hurt away. You suppress it all, you just feel nothing. Users choose drugs for that sense of belonging - that's what they did for me. You use and abuse drugs and they abuse and use you.

Cocaine Factfile

Cocaine is a drug that comes in powder form. It is also called coke or snow. The main ways to take it are sniffing or snorting (inhaling through the nose), injecting and smoking. Smoking involves inhaling cocaine vapour or smoke into the lungs where absorption into the bloodstream is as rapid as by injection. Crack cocaine is a crystalline form, which is usually smoked.

The effects:
◆ The first time it's used, many people experience a rush of pleasure (especially with crack cocaine), but they report that subsequent use fails to repeat the same 'high'.
◆ Some people feel more alert and feel they have a clearer mind.
◆ Some people feel restless, irritable and anxious.

The problems:
◆ It can cause psychological dependence and users can feel strong urges to continue using it.
◆ Taking it can cause increased temperature, heart rate and blood pressure.
◆ High doses of cocaine and/or long-term use can trigger paranoia.

◆ When dependent individuals stop using cocaine, they often become depressed. This may lead to further cocaine use to alleviate depression.
◆ People who smoke cocaine long-term may get the respiratory problems associated with smoking.
◆ Long-term cocaine snorting can damage the inner part of the nose enough to cause it to collapse.
◆ In rare instances, sudden death can occur on the first use of cocaine or unexpectedly after that.
◆ Some users alienate family and friends. They tend to become isolated and suspicious. Most of their money and time is spent getting more of the drug. The compulsion may become utterly obsessive.

Q What effect did drugs have on your personality?

A I became violent, abusive, aggressive, everything.

Q You started selling drugs. What was that like?

A It gives you power over people, other drug addicts. You think, 'I'm running things, I'm better than other junkies because I'm dealing'. At that time, I didn't care whether the police got me or whether I had to go to jail. It wasn't a worry of mine because I was on top. I thought I was cleverer than other people.

Q Did you have any drugs education at school?

A Yes, but at the Roman Catholic school I went to, they were very strict on smoking and drugs. Every week you'd get a lecture on them. But I was well into smoking cigarettes by then.

I had to go down that road, hit my rock bottom and come into treatment for me to learn by my own mistakes. School lectures - I was half asleep in them anyway.

Q Did you think you could get hooked?

A No, and I didn't accept it for a long time. People would say it gives you a good buzz and some would say that you get addicted... I had to actually find out what it does and what happens with it myself. I thought my way worked but it didn't really. I'd look at junkies and think, 'I'm not there because I wear designer clothes. I don't look like a junkie, I'm not a junkie'. At that point I didn't have a physical habit, I was

> " I'm not there because I wear designer clothes. I don't look like a junkie, I'm not a junkie. "

just using here and there. I'd see people coming up to me, people with brown teeth, not washed, and I'd think, 'They're filthy, that's not me, I'm not there'.

Q What made you realise you were an addict?

A When I started selling some of my clothes - that killed me - they were my life those clothes. That scared me because I pictured myself all scruffy, with brown teeth. I couldn't stand it and I thought, 'Rehab - I've got to get off this. I'm not going downhill anymore'.

It's a Fact that...

In the UK, 12% of 11 to 15 year olds and 30% of 15 year olds used drugs in 2001.

Q Had you seen anyone close to you become addicted?

A One of my brother's girlfriends was a drug addict as well. She used to smell and she would come and sit next to me and try to hug me. I'd push her away and say, 'You stink so don't touch me'. Soon after I could see myself losing it as well, but that's something that I couldn't do. I believe that if I'd been on it any longer I'd be injecting it... I could see it happening.

Q You were studying for a degree at the time?

A I was doing a law degree. I'd be on a page for five hours

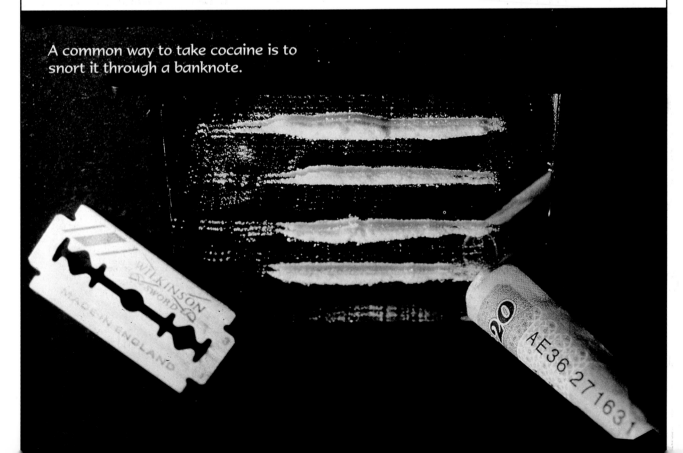

A common way to take cocaine is to snort it through a banknote.

and still not make sense of it, because of the drugs.

Q How did your family find out you were hooked?

A My sister-in-law found heroin underneath my bed.

She told my mum that she thought that I was on heroin. My mum had her suspicions but she didn't say anything. She was just too scared to find out the truth. When she did she burst into tears because of the shock, she couldn't believe that her so-called innocent sweet girl could do such a thing. For her it was like her world crumbled. She had fits and everything. She was too scared to tell my dad because she knew what he would do - give me a good beating.

Q Did your dad find out?

A We didn't tell my dad for a couple of months until I went to the clinic. Then my dad found out I was going into treatment. He said, 'All right so you're going to get help, you get help and you come back home. Or you leave home and that's it'. He was hurt that I had to use drugs.

" [My mum] couldn't believe that her so-called innocent sweet girl could do such a thing. "

It's a Fact that...

40% of people aged 16–59 have experimented with illegal drugs at least once in their lives.

> **"I like my life now better than it was. I like to be clean."**

Q What was the worst thing you did?

A The worse I ever did was to sell sentimental things - Indian gold sets, things that my mum gave me. I started selling them and my clothes. I was also stealing off my family - my dad's credit cards and stealing from my sisters.

Q What can you see in your future?

A I want to stay around here for a year or two and get myself a good job and stay with my friends here. I've made some good friends at the rehab unit. I want to stand on my feet, get a good job, get my house nice. Things like that I wouldn't think of doing back then, when I lived at home. I just relied on my mum. I'll be an independent person now. Today I want a career for myself, to come out of treatment and become a solicitor or a barrister.

Q How does it feel now that you're no longer using drugs?

A I like my life now better than it was. I like to be clean. I've got no worries and I've not got to go to punters, selling drugs. I'm not looking for my next load and my next reload. It's just a day at a time now and I'm just doing what I need to do to make a recovery. Today I must admit that I'm happy that I'm finding me. My addiction is not the only thing about me. ∎

Talking Points

◆ Why do you think it is difficult for a drug taker to recognise when drugs are taking over their life?

◆ Sanita's parents seemed to be reluctant to acknowledge her problem. Do you think it would have helped her if they had tried to deal with it earlier? Do parents have a role to play in drugs education?

◆ Sanita was not interested in school lectures on drugs education. In what other ways could she have been educated about drugs? Do you think this would have helped her?

It Happened to Martin

Martin is now 23. He is a qualified Art teacher but works as a gardener and a waiter as well as contract teaching in Melbourne, Australia. Martin started smoking cannabis when he was 13 and a student at one of the city's exclusive single-sex private schools. He stopped smoking at 15 when he had a drug-induced psychosis.

Q When did you start using cannabis?

A I was 13.

Q How did you get the money?

A I just sort of seemed to have it. My parents gave me an allowance, but it was the same amount as everyone else I knew.

Q How often were you smoking?

A Four to seven days a week. I didn't smoke at school. I'd get up, go to school and smoke after school with friends.

Q Why do you think you began smoking?

A I suppose I was one of those kids who thought he was too cool for the activities kids my age were supposed to be doing. I wasn't interested in sports. I wasn't stupid but I didn't do very well with academic studies and always did extra English and maths as remedial. I just enjoyed something exciting. At that age it's exciting to be able to know about something else.

Q Can you remember the first time you smoked cannabis?

A No - but I can remember conversations alluding to getting some. When I went to high school there were some older boys and I recall being at a house-meeting where I asked if they could get me some cannabis. They said I was too young. I don't really remember smoking it for the first time.

Q What did you get from smoking?

A It was fun... it gave me a purpose, let me engage in the environment where I was. It gave me ownership of the park and other people's houses. Different sorts of non-spaces suddenly took on a meaning when I could use them to smoke.

Cannabis Factfile

Cannabis is a brown/black resin or grass which is smoked or eaten. It is known by other names, including marijuana, ganja, weed, dope, grass, pot, resin and reefer.

The effects:
◆ Some people feel more relaxed and confident.
◆ Others feel it improves their mood and helps to keep them calm.
◆ Some people only feel dizzy and sick.
◆ It is not physically addictive.

The problems:
◆ Some regular users become constantly tired. They may lose interest in their life.
◆ Some users become paranoid.
◆ There is some evidence that suggests that long-term use causes damage to memory and concentration.
◆ Long-term use can cause lung cancer.
◆ Cannabis joints are rolled with tobacco causing some users to become addicted to tobacco and thus susceptible to its associated problems.

Q How did the drug make you feel?

A I remember being relaxed and amused but I also remember being quite often paranoid and wanting it more. It wasn't so enjoyable at times. One time, when I was 14, we had some stuff and it had horse-tranquilliser or something in it and I didn't know. I ended up thinking my friend was going to kill me.

Q Was it something to do with the forbidden aspect of it that made it attractive?

A Yes, that, and also it was exciting and different and glamorous in pop culture. In mainstream movies it's always alluded to as the cool thing that the young guy does. Even in a lot of family movies it's laughed off as a joke.

Q What were (are) your parents like?

A My father and mother are good parents. My father is a teacher and is involved in theatre and my mother is a lecturer in business and accounting. I have a sister, three years younger than me and she's studying to be a lawyer.

Q Did they know about your cannabis smoking?

A My mother did and after a while my father did too. My sister didn't and I made a conscious decision not to involve her. I didn't want her to do what I did. I didn't want to influence her because she always did quite well for herself.

Q Did you worry about getting hooked?

A No. Not at all. My dad got me some anti-drug propaganda. I read about the possible effects, like memory loss and all these little things that seemed inconsequential - apart

> **" I didn't want her [my sister] to do what I did. I didn't want to influence her because she always did quite well for herself. "**

14

> ## "I was against alcohol because on paper it looked worse than smoking cannabis."

from possible schizophrenia. You think, 'that won't be me'. Alcohol seemed far worse. I was against alcohol because on paper it looked worse than smoking cannabis.

Q Did you have many arguments?

A Yes. Screaming arguments. I remember once Dad was saying I was weak. He seemed to think it was something very weak in me, a character trait that made me do it all the time. That was awful.

Q Did you feel weak?

A At the time it felt good. It was exciting. I got to sneak out at night and smoke. I went to parties, I engaged with people I wouldn't generally engage with.

Q So why did you stop taking it?

A I had a drug-induced psychosis. I took about a year off school... and out of my life.

Q What happened?

A I stopped smoking for a month because I was sick of wanting to use all the time. The week before I was going to smoke again (and I was excited about that) I had a couple of days where I remember lying on a bed. There were about eight voices in my head, telling jokes and singing songs. I couldn't see my mother, she seemed a long way away. I also had no perception of time. Then the next day I was okay and went to school. But later I was sitting in class and the voices were in my head again.

Q What did you do?

A I asked the teacher if I could leave. They refused because they thought I was just trying to wrack off. I ended up going to the matron [school nurse] who was a good friend. All I remember then is throwing chairs and punching walls and getting quite agitated. I couldn't see reality at all because I thought what I saw was what everyone else saw. My whole perception of reality was lost.

Q What happened then?

A My mum picked me up from school that day and took me straight to a psychiatrist. She knew something was really wrong. I had a lot of drugs (to treat me), I didn't go to school and I needed 24-hour-a-day supervision.

It's a Fact that...

Cannabis is used by 2.5% of the global population (140 million people), making it the most widely used illegal drug in the world.

It's a Fact that...

The Phobic Society, a charity that supports people suffering from phobias, has seen an increase in calls from young people who link their anxieties with drug-taking. Some were long-term users, while others had experimented just once.

Q This was all related to smoking cannabis?

A Yes, the doctors thought it was a side effect of my drug-taking. The first doctor really hammered me about what drugs I'd done. He was more like a police officer.

Q Were you aggressive? And dangerous - to yourself and others?

A Very. I used to go to bed thinking I don't care if I wake up in the morning. A couple of nights I thought I'd died. I was delusional. I was pretty aggressive.

Q Do you remember much about your aggression?

A Once I was at a birthday party. All my friends said I should go home but I wanted to stay and hang out with them. My father came and he had to get me in an armlock and take me to the car. He was stopped on the street by a stranger asking if he was a police officer. He said: 'No, I'm his father'. In retrospect he's said that that was very painful for him to have to justify his actions to some stranger on the street.

On the way home I jumped out of the car and ran off. So he had to spend time walking around looking for me. I was just walking home myself by then. He said that was scary, too, looking for me. That night he slept in a bed beside my bed. He did that a few times, making sure that nothing else could go wrong.

Q What about your friends? Were they still smoking?

A Yes, they were still smoking. I wasn't smoking because of this episode.

Q Was it a choice?

A Well, not really because I wasn't really someone you could talk to. I was really out of it and on a lot of medication. I wasn't even thinking. When I did start to get better I was very upset to know that I couldn't smoke again. In an immature way, I saw that the biggest downfall of the whole event was that I

> "I used to go to bed thinking I don't care if I wake up in the morning. A couple of nights I thought I'd died."

16

Cannabis is usually rolled into a joint.

had to live the rest of my life without being able to smoke cannabis again.

Q So it was a real addiction?

A Yes. It was really upsetting. So I started drinking heavily when I was coming off medication.

Q How did your friends treat you?

A That was interesting because I had some friends who wanted to force me to smoke whilst I was very sick. Luckily I had other friends who were very vigilant against them at the time.

Q Do you think you have an addictive personality?

A Yes. I stop and start with smoking (cigarettes) and alcohol. I don't like moderation in anything. But now I'm aware of that I try to regulate it.

Q Did you ever think that this would happen to you?

A No. Never! As I said earlier I read information that this could happen. I still remember where I was sitting and who I was with when we read this - and how we scoffed at the information.

Q So you had drugs education at school?

A Yes. But it was just a forum for people to talk about what they knew about illegal drugs. It's the same with all these things. If you show kids a couple of people getting stoned certain people are immediately going to go and want to do it. It's just exciting.

Q Who helped you the most?

A My parents. They're the core of everything, even knowing when to take me straight to the doctor. Because of the relationship

I had with my mother she knew what the problem was. If I'd been secretive with them then they wouldn't have known I smoked, they wouldn't have known what the problem was. Mum had information from the start and she reacted in the best possible way from the start.

Q Do you have any regrets now?

A I had regrets then! I'd wake up and think, 'I wish I'd stop doing this'. I'd be in tears and I'd be so cross with myself I'd punch things with my fist until it bled. I was cross about how I was disappointing the people who had put so much love into me.

Q What have you learned through all of this?

A I can't say that I've 'learned' so much but I'm exceptionally glad that the episode happened, because if it hadn't happened I probably would have kept smoking. And who knows what then. Just before I got sick I ordered some designer drugs because I enjoyed smoking so much. If it hadn't happened I think I might have tried whatever there was to try and maybe my fate would have been a lot worse. I could even have ended up being a boring sort of person who smoked dope daily and had some unfulfilling job because of it. That would have been a disappointment. So I got it out of the way before university.

Cannabis is a very popular drug in many countries. Some people smoke it openly.

> **"I could even have ended up being a boring sort of person who smoked dope daily and had some unfulfilling job because of it."**

Q How do you feel about yourself and life now?

A Great. I'm very busy. Back then, I remember lying in bed a few times and having some moments where I could think properly. I was thinking that when I'm 21 - it was 21 for some reason - this will all be over, I'll be OK even though they didn't know if I was going to be OK. Now I feel I can do whatever I want.

Q Would you do drugs again?

A No, except I still enjoy tobacco and I drink alcohol, but that's the culture I'm in.

Q What would you like to say to anyone reading this?

A Try to be as informed as you can. Make your own decisions about what you're going to get out of the short and the long term. For me that year was the worst-ever part of my life and I hated every minute of it. I definitely wouldn't advise using drugs. It takes away all your energy. Some people are supposed to be able to function forever on it. I've yet to see anyone functioning like that in the way they should be. I don't think it's a viable option for anyone. ∎

Talking Points

◆ Martin says he was not into sport at school. A recent study looked at drug-taking and lifestyle among 15 year olds. They found teenagers who took part in sport were less likely to use drugs. Teenagers who were offenders were more likely to take drugs. Why do you think doing sport or being an offender makes a difference?

◆ Before taking cannabis Martin decided that alcohol has worse effects. Why do you think he thought this? Do you agree?

◆ In some countries cannabis is a legal drug, in others it is illegal. Do you think it should be a legal drug? Why?

◆ Do you think there is such a thing as an addictive personality? Are some people 'immune' from becoming addicted to things?

It Happened to Rachel

Rachel, 21, was a drug user for 10 years. She has two young sons, aged one and three, who live with their father's mother. Their father is in prison for drug offences.

Q When did you start using?

A When I was 11. I started with gas and alcohol. I was using cannabis at 13 and by the time I was 15 it was ecstasy and amphetamines. At 16 I was injecting heroin, and using crack cocaine. And it carried on like that until now, so I've been injecting drugs for five years.

Q How did you get the money for drugs?

A I've done everything. I stole off families, shoplifted, burglaries and prostitution. I've sold drugs, mainly ecstasy and I sold heroin. Anything that you can do, you will do. Anything at all.

Q You used to live with your boyfriend. Was he using as well?

A He had a drug habit before but he was clean at the time. He didn't have a heroin addiction but he was taking ecstasy and alcohol. I thought because he wasn't using heroin at the time that he was clean. I didn't understand you have to be off all drugs to be clean.

Heroin Factfile

Heroin is a drug made from morphine, a naturally occurring substance taken from the seedpod of the Asian poppy plant. It usually appears as a white or brown powder. Street names for heroin include smack, gear, H, skag and junk.

The effects:
◆ Heroin gives the user a feeling of warmth and well-being. He or she may also feel more self-confident and 'loved'.
◆ Following this initial 'high', some users feel alternately wakeful and drowsy. The brain becomes clouded.

The problems:
◆ Heroin is associated with serious health conditions, including fatal overdose, pregnancy problems and collapsed veins.
◆ Sharing needles with other users when injecting heroin can lead to HIV/AIDS.
◆ With regular heroin use, tolerance develops. This means the abuser must use more heroin to achieve the same effect.

◆ As higher doses are used over time, physical dependence and addiction develop. With physical dependence, the body has adapted to the presence of the drug and withdrawal symptoms may occur if use is reduced or stopped.
◆ Withdrawal leads to drug craving, restlessness, muscle and bone pain, insomnia, diarrhoea and vomiting, cold flashes with goose bumps ('cold turkey'), kicking movements ('kicking the habit') and other symptoms. These can be so bad that people go back to using, even though they no longer get any benefits from the drug.
◆ Heroin is very expensive, and addicts can spend all of their time trying to get hold of money just to buy it.

Q Did you have any drugs education at school?

A The police came in to do ours. We were all sat like, 'Yeah, whatever' - you know, not taking a blind bit of notice. We were already smoking, drinking and all that then so we were thinking, 'You haven't got a clue'. Really the police didn't have a clue. They just used to say drugs are bad - that's it. And if you tell that to a kid they're going to say, 'Right! We're going to try it!' That's what you do.

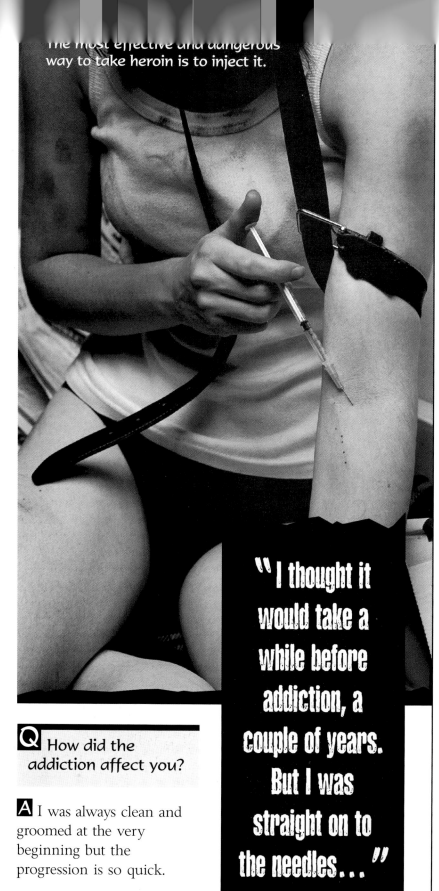

The most effective and dangerous way to take heroin is to inject it.

Q Did you think you'd get hooked?

A My boyfriend, my children's dad, he had already been hooked so I knew you could get a physical habit. But I didn't know how quickly. I saw heroin addicts on the street and I really believed that they were just weak people. I thought I was strong-minded so it wouldn't get me. I believed I was strong because I'd survived all this stuff through my childhood and I was still all right - I thought. I was 'all right' but I was drinking, I was smoking, I was taking Es and cocaine and amphetamines. I just hadn't picked up crack and heroin.

Q What happened when you started taking crack and heroin?

A I thought it would take a while before addiction, a couple of years. But I was straight on to the needles and got a habit really, really quickly. I used to slag prostitutes off and think no-one needs to do that. And then a couple of years later I was doing it myself. You always believe that you'll never get there but you always will, you really will.

Q How did the addiction affect you?

A I was always clean and groomed at the very beginning but the progression is so quick.

"I thought it would take a while before addiction, a couple of years. But I was straight on to the needles…"

22

You can hide it at first. Before I wouldn't leave the house without doing my hair and make-up. But eventually I had long straggly hair, all split and I weighed about 53 kilograms. My clothes hung off me and they were filthy, absolutely filthy. One day you look in the mirror and you're all right. The next day you look in the mirror and you think, 'Oh, my god'. But it doesn't stop you, you just carry on again.

Q What do you think you lost through drugs?

A I was training to be a dental nurse. I lost that. I've got two beautiful boys, I don't have them with me now. I only have contact with my boys in a family centre for an hour. I lost all my family, none of them would speak to me. I lost my self-respect. Nobody wants to talk to you when you're walking around half dead and they don't know if you're going to pinch the purse from their pocket. I lost all the love that I had around me. Christmases, birthdays, all the happy times - you never get them on drugs. My granddad died, I didn't grieve his death. I put both my children through hell and back because I was on drugs.

"I've got two beautiful boys, I don't have them with me now..."

Q What did your family say when they realised you were hooked?

A They didn't really notice the ecstasy. Until you get to heroin, being on drugs doesn't seem to be recognised. It's not seen as a problem, even though it is. Anyway, when I started on heroin, my mum used to come round and say, 'What's up with you?' She knew I wasn't right. I used to say, 'Nothing, nothing'. You get so devious and so sneaky. You could blag a nun into giving you her knickers, you could. You're so sly you can hide it for a long, long time. My mum said to me, 'You're taking drugs'. I denied it. They didn't find out for sure until my first baby was born. He was born heroin-dependent.

Q What happened then?

A My mum stopped speaking to me for a bit. My grandma and the father's family helped, because of the baby. They didn't really go mad; because yelling in your face: I didn't give a monkey's. If you can't stop using when you have to watch your baby withdraw from heroin, you won't stop because your family shout at you.

Q What made you look for help?

A I had both my kids taken off me. I was a complete mess. I tried many different attempts and many different ways to stop. When my boyfriend was in prison I'd try and get off but soon as he came back out I'd be back on again. I'd go to see my boys, come back and I'd be so depressed and suicidal. I just didn't want to live any more. I banged my head off of brick walls. I'd be going to drugs projects for years in my home town. One day I went in and said, 'Listen, I need to go into rehab. There's just no other way for me. It's either change what I'm doing, get my boys back or I might as well take an overdose and die.' I was just in the pits of despair. I couldn't handle it any more. It really had me on my knees.

> " I know it's not all going to be rosy but that's what I want out of life - to be happy, really happy, not from drugs. "

It's a Fact that...

In the UK 15% of 11 year olds and 61% of 15 year olds were offered drugs in 2001.

Q Was it difficult to get into rehab?

A They did an assessment for me to come into treatment. For 16 weeks I had to go in three times a week and get through an assessment. I had to show dedication because it costs a lot of money to fund you through rehab. You need to show dedication to it first. So I showed dedication and motivation and I was enthusiastic about it. But I'd go in and they'd said it was going to be another week. Every time I was like, 'I can't hold on any longer'. But I did. I had to get to that state before I could finally give up. I'm glad I've come into rehab. I'm sick of it sometimes, but I'm glad I'm here.

Q What's helped you?

A The fact that I've got two beautiful boys. I know I am going to get them back one day and live a normal, clean life. I'm finding out all sorts about myself. I'm learning to like myself and be comfortable with me and what I need. I don't feel the need to have a man in my life. I'm learning to be able to cope on my own with two boys. I know it's not all going to be rosy but that's what I want out of life - to be happy, really happy, not from drugs. Drugs only make you happy for the first few months and then you're not happy at all.

Q Did your boyfriend go back to using?

A Yes, and when he started back on it he got into a terrible state really quickly. That's what happens, when you start back on it you progress really quickly and your appearance deteriorates so quickly. So you could see it in his face and in his physical appearance.

Q Does he see your sons?

A He's in prison at the moment. He'll get out of prison in December and he's going straight into a job. He doesn't know about total abstinence. As he's going into a job he'll have money and he'll want to go out and start using again. There's no future for us really - not as partners. Friendship probably and parents to our children - that's all.

Q What do you feel about yourself and your life now?

A I like to know that I have the chance for a normal life - - being able even to just do my hair and my make-up and take the kids to school, come home and cook the tea. To other people that might be boring. To me that's something different to

> " I like to know that I have the chance for a normal life... "

It's a Fact that...

In England 1% of 11 year olds and 23% of 15 year olds are regular smokers.

what I did before. I have thoughts of what I can do in the future in my career. I might have said it in the past but I wouldn't really think I could ever get there.

Q How does it feel to be off drugs now?

A It's not having them over your head in the morning when you wake up. There's nothing worse than waking up rattling - when you're really ill and thinking, 'Oh god, what have I got to do today to get those drugs?' You can't do anything if you're rattling, but you can't get gear because you're rattling. It's a vicious circle all the time.

Q What about your future?

A I'd like to become a counsellor, particularly with mothers who are addicts. I'd let them know that they're not on their own and that I've been there and there is a

way out. I'm finding a love for my children that I never thought I had. My idea of love was dragging them around into smack dealers' dens and injecting drugs in front of them and giving them the odd cuddle on the sofa or buying them toys. I'd never experienced love, so

how was I supposed to give it to them? But now I'm learning how I tick, why I tick, and to like myself.

Q What would you say to other young people about drugs?

A You do enjoy them at the start. But don't ever think, 'It'll never hurt me. It'll never get to me'. It only makes you happy for the first few months and then you're not happy at all. You may think you are different to anyone else but nobody is different to heroin, nobody, believe me. ■

Talking Points

◆ Rachel and her friends were already drinking and smoking by the time they had drugs education in school. When do you think is the right time to be discussing this subject? What should pupils be told about drugs in school? Who do you think should do drugs education – teachers, the police, doctors or someone else?

◆ Rachel mentions 'total abstinence' because the rehab treatment centre she goes to does not allow her to use any drugs at all, including alcohol. Why do you think this is the rule? Would it make it easier or harder for her to stay off heroin?

It Happened to Chris*

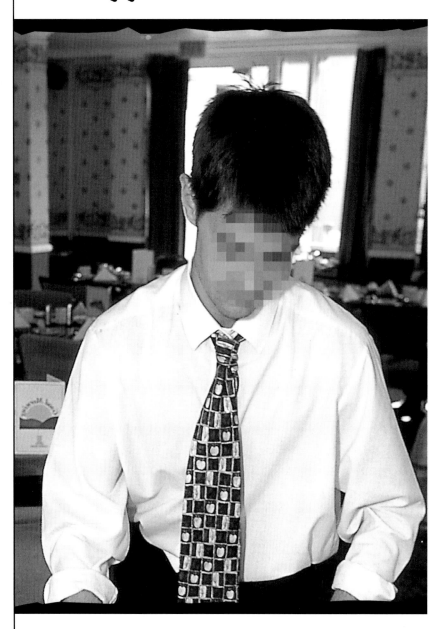

Chris is in his early thirties and started using drugs in his early twenties. He has a successful career as a company director. He lives with his partner and two children. He enjoys using drugs and, at the moment, has no intentions to stop using them.
* Not his real name.

Q When did you start using?

A I had a few goes at university when I was a student living with some very boring other students. But I missed the 'Summer of Love' (1989) by a mile and only ended up using regularly once I moved to London properly in 1994.

Q What do you use?

A Mostly ecstasy. I've used some cocaine, some hash [cannabis], some LSD, some magic mushrooms, occasional speed.

Q Do you use much now?

A Occasionally, although I have a family now so I always have to get a babysitter. When I first started, most of the people I lived with were all health freaks, but this was good as it tempered my habits. I never thought I could get hooked and I haven't.

Q Did you have drugs education at school ?

A Yes. It was a police officer giving a talk. It made

drugs seem brilliant as there was absolutely nothing bad that the guy could say about either hash or LSD. He didn't mention ecstasy as it wasn't common at that time. He told us about the dangers of heroin and other hard drugs, but we were absolutely dying to go and try the 'safe' drugs.

Q How does ecstasy affect you?

A People often use the term 'rush' and I think that is very descriptive. Ecstasy gives you a sort of rush of energy, but not like coffee or amphetamines. This is a sort of intense emotional rush, mixed with love and well-being. At night-clubs a lot of people take ecstasy, but I always prefer to take it before entering the club to make the waiting in queues more bearable. Frankly, on E, even if a mad axe murderer ran at you, you would

Ecstasy Factfile

Ecstasy, scientific name MDMA, is a chemically produced drug, coming as tablets, capsules or occasionally powders. The look of the tablets and capsules changes all the time as producers try to evade the law. Street names include E, doves, rhubarb and custard, shamrocks, plus many more.

The effects:
◆ It may give strong feelings of empathy or even love for people around the user.
◆ It increases heart rate and keeps the user awake for long periods – so it is popular with clubbers.
◆ It is not physically addictive, although some people take more and more because the everyday becomes boring to them.

The problems:
◆ It can cause a dry mouth and throat and raise blood pressure.
◆ Once the drug has worn off it may cause tiredness and depression, but usually only temporarily.
◆ The user cannot be sure what is in a tablet. It's likely to be cut with other substances, for example Ketamine (an anaesthetic) or methadone (a heroin substitute).
◆ Sudden deaths have occurred through using ecstasy, although this is rare – direct effects of the drug can cause heart attacks or brain haemorrhages. Indirectly people may die from drinking too much water, causing the brain to swell, and also from heat-stroke.
◆ Long-term use may cause brain impairment (e.g. memory loss, slower thinking skills, depression), but the full effects, are not yet known.

probably just turn around and give him a great big hug and a smile. As I have grown older and more responsible in my daily life, the rushes seem less carefree and there is a certain sordid quality about using E now. I guess I just feel a bit dated for all of this, and this affects the mood that the drug gives you. I really have to be on top form to take it now, and I would advise anybody who uses the drug to always make sure of their psychological well-being before going for it.

Q What was it like the first time you used?

A The feeling was out of this world. We were young people surrounded by friendship and love with not a care in the world and the E just amplified this.

Q Why did you go on using?

A For two reasons. One, I am a pleasure seeker and I need to make the best of my time outside work, so I use drugs to increase the intensity. This is especially true since I have a very stressful job now. The second is that I think there are two teams in life, one that takes

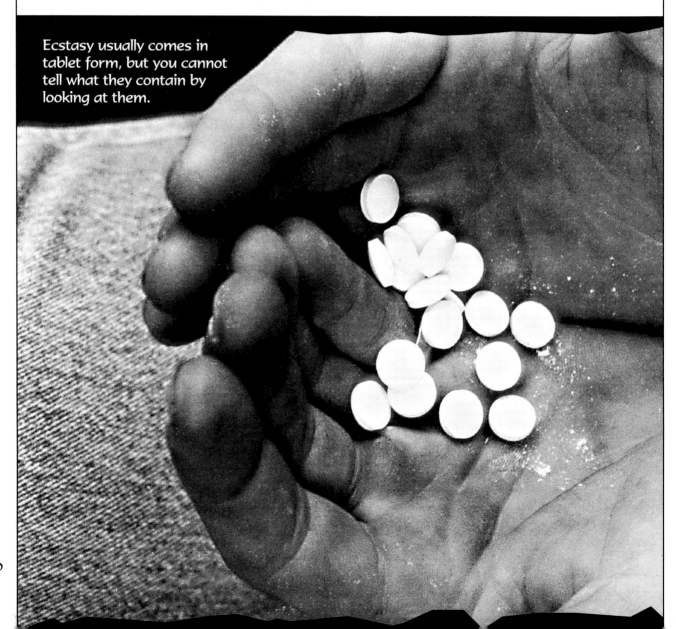

Ecstasy usually comes in tablet form, but you cannot tell what they contain by looking at them.

It's a Fact that...

In Holland the police and night-clubs work together to reduce the risks. They even test the pills and allow people to take three in to the club. In 2001 Holland had no ecstasy deaths.

and one that does not. You are either with one or the other and I am with the former.

Q Where do you get your drugs from?

A Generally, other people get it for me and I pay them back. I don't consume enough to really have a 'dealer'.

Q How do you get the money for it?

A Hard work. No, sorry, I don't conform to the 'drug-addict steals grandma's handbag' stereotype.

Q How do you feel about the fact that drug-taking is illegal?

A I'm not harming anyone, or acting irresponsibly in day-to-day life. I see no

problem. Alcohol is a drug and so is tea or coffee or cigarettes or half the stuff you find in health shops and pharmacies. It is just an arbitrary, legal aberration that so-called 'recreational drugs' are illegal and there is nothing immoral or wrong about them.

Q Did you ever worry about getting hooked?

A I was never hooked, but I imagine that the rave life-style is something which can become a habit. Some people live their whole lives just to spend six hours in some club on E. That's not for me.

Q What has been the worst thing to happen to you while using?

A A friend once freaked out. She took too much and

started to hallucinate. But I steered her clear of traffic and she was physically okay.

Q Have you ever done anything on E you regret?

A Well, the drug does make you a little bit randy... so I have two kids now, but I don't regret a thing!

Q Has your drug-taking ever caused problems with friends or you life in general?

A Not at all. On the contrary, friends have

" I would advise anybody who uses the drug to always make sure of their psychological well-being before going for it."

31

It's a Fact that...

Statistics show that most ecstasy users don't go on to use 'harder', more dangerous drugs and most people stop using it in their twenties.

Regular ecstasy users are 25% more likely to suffer a mental health disorder than the rest of the population.

become soul mates – I really only take drugs with my best friends. It has never affected my working life or my relationships or getting on with my family.

could give me one shred of evidence of the long-term harm that E does. Everything I've seen doesn't convince me. Most of the people I know use the way I do which means nobody has ever given me a hard time about what I do. I work really hard and pay my way. Using the occasional E is just my way of relaxing and harming no-one, least of all myself.

Q What would make you stop using?

A I would stop using completely if somebody

Q What have you learned?

A That some things in life that are outlawed or

Ecstasy is associated with 'club culture'.

> ## " I work really hard and pay my way. Using the occasional E is just my way of relaxing... "

Some people feel tired and depressed after taking ecstasy.

stigmatised are really worth having. I wouldn't change anything - not a thing. I'm very happy with myself and with my life. In spite of my subversion, I have achieved a great deal for my years.

Q How do you see your future?

A I have a good future. I am not a drug addict but a drug user - there's a great difference.

Q What would you like to say to anyone reading this?

A Everything in moderation. Just avoid those drugs that do not permit moderation such as heroin and cocaine. ■

Talking Points

◆ Chris believes responsible adults should have the right to take drugs if they want to. Do you agree or is it right that governments direct what people can and can't do with their bodies?

◆ Chris didn't start taking drugs until he was in his twenties. Is this why he seems to have handled them responsibly or do you think it is more to do with his personality... or has he been lucky?

◆ Do you think it makes a difference that Chris is now a parent? Should this change his drug-taking or not? How do you think his partner might feel about it? What if the next ecstasy pill were polluted?

ST STEPHEN'S SCHOOL
CARRAMAR

It Happened to Hannah*

Hannah, 30, works as an office manager for an international company. She has been experimenting with different drugs on and off since she was a teenager, but she now prefers not to take any.
* Not her real name.

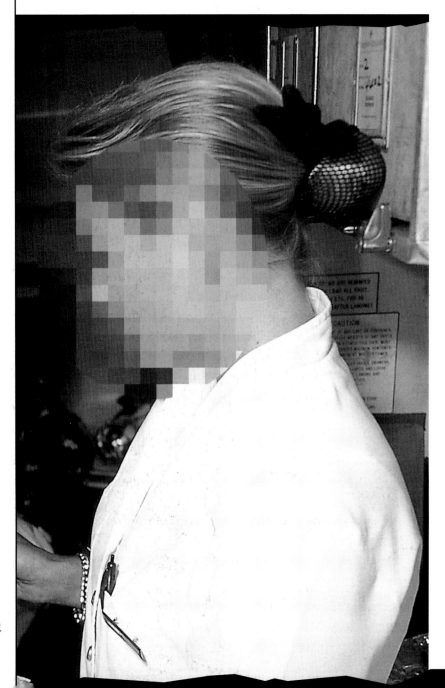

Q When was the first time you used a drug and what was it?

A I was 18 and smoked [cannabis] resin with my first serious boyfriend. He was seven years older than me and I trusted him. I wasn't really scared, he was a good friend and knew it was my first time. He watched the whole time and it was little and in small doses rather than all or nothing.

Q Why did you take it?

A I wanted to know what it was like. A lot of my friends had taken it and I'd always been 'younger' and therefore never offered it. I'm sure my parents had taken it when they were younger - the whole 'sixties' thing - and I was curious.

From the age of 18 to 22 god knows how much I was smoking. Then I had a two-year gap then smoked again, but more controlled. It was more of a luxury than a necessity. I really don't enjoy it now, it makes me ill - so I don't do it.

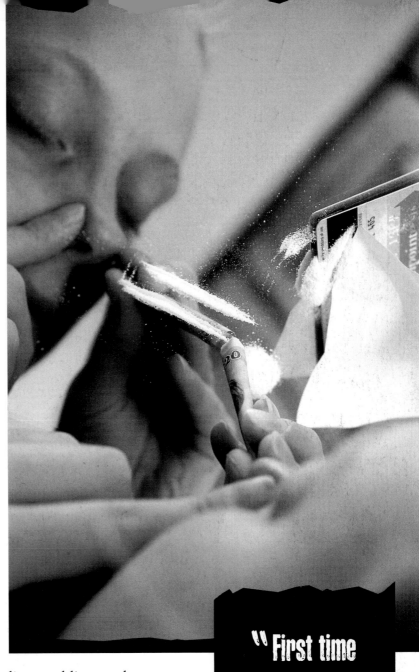

Q What else have you used?

A Speed, cocaine, ecstasy and magic mushrooms.

Q What were these drugs like?

A Speed's the best drug for getting you going, giving confidence and not impairing your speech or coordination. Lethal, though! You never knew what mix you were getting. I first took it when I was 19 - loved it and couldn't get enough. God, it's foul though. Just thinking about it now makes me want to retch, because that's what you do. It hits the back of the throat when you snort it and then slowly starts dripping down. The taste is vile - it's like ammonia in the back of your throat.

Q Did you enjoy cocaine more then?

A Cocaine, I'm afraid, I still describe as a great drug. Would never take it again, but still get the urge. It is truly addictive - I should know. First time I took it was at a party where they had a mirrored table, I've never forget it. There was lines and lines and as soon as I took a line, god I knew the difference. I never went back to speed.

Q And the ecstasy?

A First time I took E was quite a funny experience. A friend knew it was my

> **"First time I took it was at a party where they had a mirrored table, never forget it."**

35

> **" I got trapped on the loo for an hour because the carpet was running under the loo and I thought that if I put my feet down I'd go with it. "**

first time - I've always been honest about that and never ashamed. Everybody needs to start somewhere. We got this E and took half each, then we were supposed to get ready and go out. But for five hours, apart from drinking pints and pints of water, we were actually taking it in turns to throw up. It's a wonder we lived. By the time we were okay to go out it was six in the morning and it was time to get ready for work. We both found it hilarious!

Q **What were magic mushrooms like?**

A Magic mushrooms - a great, great drug. But it can go horribly wrong. I got trapped on the loo for an hour because the carpet was running under the loo and I thought that if I put my feet down I'd go with it. I was 'saved' in the end by my two friends breaking the door down and putting towels on the floor to help me out.

Q Why did you go on using?

A I enjoyed experimenting. There were so many experiences which I wouldn't do now. Going clubbing and getting completely lost in the music and dancing for hours and hours on end. Playing Monopoly for 48 hours without stopping. Lying and looking at the stars and feeling yourself lifting and flying with the stars. I had the most amazing trips, lucky for me. I also had bad ones but the bad ones I accepted and brought back down to earth when they were happening. The good ones I went with. They were great.

Q What were the bad trips like?

A Everyone remembers their first real hangover. Well, imagine that three-fold and then take away the numbness.

Because you'll feel everything - take away the ability to sleep through it (because you won't be able to), add the feeling of being starving (but you won't be able to eat). Just imagine two runny eggs and a jam doughnut - throw in a pounding heart, hot and cold sweats to the extreme, the inability to move and anxiety like you have never had before - and you're close to a bad trip. Not the worst you can have, but it's halfway there.

Q Did you ever worry that you might get hooked?

A Yes, because I never thought I'd be hooked by smoking and I was.

Q Were drugs ever a problem?

A I think they have affected my health. I still have to work harder at getting my body on

> **"I think they have affected my health. I still have to work harder at getting my body on track."**

track. Drugs aren't for one night, they can be for life.

Q Do you still use anything?

A No, I don't. I still have that urge, but don't have the desire - there's a big difference. There's been too much water under the bridge and too much pain inbetween. I had a wake-up call when I had a breakdown. I lost my soul for a few weeks and it scares me. The drugs must have added to the pressure. I will never forget that experience. I regret the things I said and did to my close family and friends through this time. Nothing is more painful that looking back - for this reason I have no desire to do drugs again.

It's a Fact that...

A ten-year study in Holland concluded that cannabis use does not lead to the use of hard drugs such as cocaine and heroin.

It's a Fact that...

Giving up cocaine, although not pleasant, is not as difficult as quitting heroin as it has few physical withdrawal symptons.

It's hard though as I had so many good times when taking drugs. You feel like you need a vice!

Q What would you have liked to have been different?

A I would like to have been given the confidence at school that it's okay to be different, to have your own ideas and to have been helped to develop them. This would probably have given me the confidence to say no, although I would still have experimented. I don't think I was ever really silly at taking drugs. I knew when my body had had enough and would always stop.

Q What have you learned about using drugs?

A It's for life. The consequences can take years but they appear at some point, in some form. If you are going to do it, which some people will no matter what anyone says to them, make sure you are aware of what to expect and what to do if things go wrong. Make sure it's from a trusted source and you do it with someone you trust and who is experienced. It sounds mad but it might just save you.

Cocaine (top left) is a white powder usually sold in paper packets. The other drugs are cannabis (bottom left) and heroin - in the foil.

Q So it's all about knowledge and trusting people?

A Yes. I am also very tuned to my body, I can almost immediately tell if something is not right and always asked in advance the 'what if' questions. My lesson? Know your friends, talk about it beforehand. Become clear on the downs (the real downs), what to expect, how it made them feel and what experience they had on their first time, their worst experience on that particular substance and how they managed to work themselves through it. They say knowledge can be dangerous, yes it can, but I know it can also be a saviour!

Q Do you regret the past?

A I did things I regretted, but we all make mistakes. I can't look back and carry the guilt with me. You have to move on. I think it's part of growing up - you make your choices and if you're lucky you can move on and start to really appreciate things. Yes, there are things I'd wished I'd done, but it's not too late.

Q What would you like to say to anyone reading this?

A I can't say don't do it, because if you want to you will and that's why taking care is important. Now answer the question, is it worth it? You'd be an idiot if you answered yes, because you probably wouldn't survive and if you do, what are you left with? If in doubt - don't. You are a stronger and more respected person for saying 'no'.

Having your period, drinking too much, sleepless nights, partying too hard can all affect the outcome. You have to remember that you are an individual and unique. If the time isn't right, don't -

" [Drugs are] for life. The consequences can take years but they appear at some point, in some form."

there's a reason for it and there will always be another opportunity if it's right. You only have to ask someone that's had a bad 'trip' and they will say the same; when it's bad - it can be really bad. ■

Talking Points

◆ Hannah used drugs over a long period without getting completely addicted. How do you think she managed this?

◆ Hannah paid for her drugs out of her own pocket and didn't injure anyone directly by taking drugs. If she had been caught taking drugs, do you think she should she have been punished as the law demands?

It Happened to Bob

Bob's 12 years of substance and drug abuse ended in the death of his father. Instead of a prison sentence he went into a drug addiction treatment centre. At the time of this interview he had been there eight months (see factfile opposite).

Q When did you start using?

A I started sniffing gas [solvents] at age of 8, then smoking cannabis at 11. At 13 I got into heroin. I went into prison when I was 15 and when I came out started crack and got back into heroin.

Q How did drugs make you feel?

A I never got love and I never got acceptance as a child. What I got from drugs was confidence and acceptance, I got love from it basically. I started to love myself when I was using. I thought I was Jack the lad, you know, I had power and control over people. I felt like I was walking down the street and I was owning it. It gave me self-worth. Drugs gave me gifts to do everything I wanted to do, that I was never able to do before. For example, I couldn't speak up to someone in front of 30 people but it gave me that confidence... I worshipped drugs. When you're high, whatever comes in your way - a brick wall, whatever - you'll come through that.

Factfile - Drug Addiction Treatment (Rehab)

What is drug addiction treatment?

There are many addictive drugs, and treatments for specific drugs differ. Treatment also varies depending on the characteristics of the patient. People who are addicted to drugs come from all walks of life. Some suffer from health or social problems that make their addiction more difficult to treat.

Treatment usually includes counselling and / or medication. Drug users look at strategies for coping with their drug cravings, learn ways to avoid drugs and prevent relapse or deal with relapse if it occurs. Counselling may look at the development of self-awareness, to allow each patient to explore their own addictive behaviour.

Why can't drug addicts quit without help?

Nearly all addicts believe at first that they can stop using drugs on their own, without help. However, most of these attempts result in failure to achieve long-term abstinence. Research has shown that long-term drug use results in significant changes in the brain that continue long after the person stops using drugs. This may make them go back to drug use, even though it could harm them.

How effective is drug addiction treatment?

According to several studies, drug addiction treatment reduces drug use by 40 to 60% and significantly decreases criminal activity during and after treatment.

How long does drug addiction treatment usually last?

Individuals progress through drug addiction treatment at various speeds. Generally, however, studies have shown that participation for less than 90 days is of limited or no effectiveness. Many treatments can last a year or longer.

What helps people stay in treatment?

Whether a patient stays in treatment depends primarily on the individual's commitment to it. He or she has to be motivated to stop drug using and needs support from family and friends. There may also be pressure to stay in treatment from the criminal justice system or child protection services.

Q Why did you use so many different drugs?

A I used gas for at least two years. I used to love using it. I'd have hallucinations - things like trees flying at me. I stopped using gas because someone told me I'd freeze my lungs up. I found another drug - cannabis. I found that really good, mixing with people and going into pubs and clubs. I could get cannabis easily. But it stopped giving me a buzz and I needed something else. I needed something to progress the feelings. Heroin was really, I thought, the drug I was looking for all my life. But after I started using heroin my life became totally messed up.

Q What happened to you?

A After the first month of using heroin my life was totally unmanageable. That's how low my addiction took me. You've got no dress sense and you just want your fix. I wouldn't have breakfast in the morning, I was bang on gear straight away - that's my breakfast for the whole day. If I couldn't get it, I'd fight to get it.

> " Heroin was really, I thought, the drug I was looking for all my life."

From the age of 14, I've been to prison many times and I'm sick of it. I tried killing myself because of heroin. I used to make cuts on my arms. I'm surprised I'm still alive.

Bob began his drug-taking, like this boy, with solvent abuse.

It's a Fact that...

Cannabis is the most likely illegal drug to be used, by 11% of 11 to 14 year olds and 28% of 15 year olds. Fewer than 0.5% of 11 to 15 year olds had used heroin but 3% had tried a stimulant such as ecstasy, cocaine, crack, amphetamines or poppers.

Q Did you have any drugs education at school?

A I didn't take any notice. I was off my head. In the playground I'd have a little smoke, come back in and be stoned. I was a joker at school, the class clown. I didn't take any notice of things like that. What finally got my attention was when police officers put me in a cell. That's how I realised this is my life - in a prison cell. That hit my head more than a lecture. I didn't believe in lectures at the time. I believe in lectures now and I take them in because I know that I need to stay sober and clean.

Q Did you think you'd get hooked?

A No. I knew that there were consequences of getting hooked but not for me. I saw all my mates rattling and dying skinny and I used to call them things, names, I used to call them tramps. And it turns out I was one of them. I never thought I'd turn out to be one of them. I couldn't believe it!

Q How did you pay for your drugs?

A From 8 to 9 I was into shoplifting. I had a little bike and a rucksack. I went into shops and took charity boxes. I used to put them in the bag and ride off on my getaway bike. From then on I always had a lot of money on me. I started spending a lot of money on gas cans. I used to say it was for my dad, or blag them.

From the age of 11 I used to hang around people 10 years older than me. They accepted me because I had a background - burgling houses, breaking into churches and robbing from temples. I'd take £100 a day from my mum and that wasn't enough. I had to street-rob old people. I find it hard to say that now because I'm not like that today. But I was eight months ago. I was doing really severe damage to old people, pushing them around and doing handbag snatches.

Q Was that the worst thing you did on drugs?

A When I couldn't get drugs I would hurt people

> " ... it turns out I was one of them. I never thought I'd turn out to be one of them [an addict]. I couldn't believe it!"

43

Bob began the long road to recovery at a drugs rehabilitation unit.

next morning. The worst thing was seeing my dad's body with machines pumped in his chest and not even feeling a thing.

Q What did your family say when they realised you were hooked?

A My mum chucked me out of the house and disowned me because of the embarrassment. My mum was terrified. She didn't want to chuck me out, but it was getting too much for her. My dad was alive at that time and when he found out he started beating me up. He was angry about it. I was angry as well that they chucked me out. I couldn't understand why they did that.

Q What do you think you lost through drugs?

A I've lost a lot of things in life that I can't get back. I lost my dad - that was the biggest thing in my life I lost. And I hurt my mum. I lost my brother's love, my sister's love, I lost people respecting me. And I lost my career, opportunities and college. I wanted to be a computer engineer. My brother, he's got degrees. I wanted to be like

because I was a coward. I was picking on vulnerable people, old people off the street. I went to prison for that. When I came back out I started doing it to my family.

Q What happened?

A My dad became ill, and I started picking on him for his pension money. On New Year's Eve I smacked a bottle on him and I beat him up. He was dead at 11 o'clock the

> ## "I came in here like a boy, and I'm going out like a man now. Responsible."

him - I lost all that. My family completely disowned me, people were embarrassed to walk around with me.

Q What made you look for help?

A I was going to get a life sentence in prison and I cried for help. I got sick of the drugs. Using was just backfiring in my face. I tried slitting my wrists. I'd just had enough of it. I couldn't live with using. I went for sentencing in court and the court sent me here, a drugs rehabilitation unit.

Q Are your family supportive?

A Not at first. My brother put me in prison for my dad's death and then disowned me. But now I've got so much support from them it's unbelievable. My

mum phones me every night. I can be with my family now because they are supportive. They will sit there and have time for me to express how I feel. They can see how well I'm doing.

Q How long have you been clean?

A It's been eight months. I'm giving back to society with voluntary work. I'm working for free in charity shops and painting and decorating. I'm only 20, I came in here like a boy, and I'm going out like a man now. Responsible.

Q Do you feel more hope now you're in rehab?

A I'm working towards it now. I'm in the right place

and doing the right things. Now I feel I can't go wrong. I keep talking, expressing how I feel, instead of covering it up as I used to. I'm cooking my own food and everything. I'm happy with myself, but I had to work on that.

Q What will you do when you leave rehab?

A I would like to go into schools and share my experiences with children. I do that in meetings now. I'm going to prisons and sharing my life experiences in front of 300 people. I'm getting in there and giving back to society because I hurt society so much. I'm volunteering around this area now. I'm giving back for free, because I feel it's what I need to do. ■

Talking Points

◆ Bob's addiction turned him to crime. What if drugs were legal and free? Do you think society would be safer and would it be worth it? (What's more important, a safer community or protecting people from drugs?)

◆ Bob thought drugs could fix his unhappiness. Do you think drugs can help people who are unhappy? How might they change things without using drugs?

Useful addresses and contacts

UK

Your own doctor

National Drugs Helpline
A 24-hour freephone number for queries or concerns regarding drugs.

0800 776600

Drugscope
A leading UK centre of expertise on drugs with links to other organisations around the world.

Waterbridge House
32-36 Loman Street
London SE1 0EE
(www.drugscope.org.uk)

020 7928 1211

Narcotics Anonymous
For recovering drug addicts.
202 City Road
London EC1V 2PH
(www.ukna.org)

Helpline: 020 7730 0009

Re-solv
Information about solvent and volatile substance abuse.

(www.re-solv.org)

Helpline: 0808 800 2345

Scotland Against Drugs
A joint initiative from the leading political parties.

120 Bath Street
Glasgow G2 2EN
(www.sad.org.uk)

0141 331 6150

Trashed
A website where you can get information about drug effects, UK law and what to do in an emergency.

(www.trashed.co.uk)

ADFAM National
For drug users and their families and friends.

Waterbridge House
32-36 Loman St
London SE1 0EE

Office: 020 7928 8898
Helpline: 020 7928 8900

Youth Access
Local youth advisory services. For your nearest contact:

1-2 Taylors Yard
67 Alderbrook Road
London SW12 8AD

Office: 020 8772 9900

D-2K
An interactive website that informs about the risks of drug use through an interactive street story. You can find out about the law, ask questions and get answers from the hotline team.

(www.d-2k.co.uk)

The Site
Website offering advice on youth centres near you plus information on drugs.

(www.thesite.org.uk)

AUSTRALIA

Australian Drug Federation
An organisation working to prevent and reduce alcohol and drug problems.

409 King Street
West Melbourne
VIC 3003
(www.adf.org.au)

(03) 9278 8100

Glossary

More information is given on some of the drugs listed below in factfiles as indicated. This is only a starting point for finding out about these drugs. If you are thinking about taking anything, make sure you are as informed as possible by looking at the websites or contacting the organisations listed on page 46.

abstinence When no drugs are taken at all.

addict Someone who feels a physical or mental need to do something, such as take drugs.

amphetamine A stimulant drug that comes in powder or tablet form. Also called speed.

cannabis A brown/black resin or grass which is smoked or eaten. It is known by many other names, including marijuana, ganja, weed, dope, hash, grass, pot, resin and reefer. Also see page 13.

cocaine A drug that comes in powder form. It is also called coke or snow. Also see page 7.

crack A crystalline and very strong form of cocaine that is usually smoked. Also called base.

delusional Believing in a mistaken idea.

designer drug A drug, for example ecstasy, that has been created using chemicals.

downers (tranquillisers) These come in capsules or tablets. They help to calm people down and may provide temporary relief from tension or fear. They are prescribed by a doctor, and selling them for use as a recreational drug is illegal.

Heavy users of one type, not usually prescribed any more (barbiturates), may suffer from bronchitis, pneumonia or hypothermia. Tranquilliser use often leads to tolerance and dependence, unpleasant symptoms when the user comes off the drug, and accidental overdose.

ecstasy A tablet-form drug with stimulant and hallucinogenic effects. Also called E or MDMA. Also see page 29.

gas A chemical solvent that is breathed in by the user. The effect can be heightened by using a plastic bag held over the mouth or nose. Solvent abuse is extremely dangerous and can be fatal.

hallucinogenic A type of drug that alters the way the user sees and hears things.

heroin A drug made from morphine, a naturally occurring substance taken from the seedpod of the Asian poppy plant. It usually appears as a white or brown powder. Also called smack, gear, H, skag, and junk. Also see page 21.

junkie A slang term for a drug addict.

load A slang term for a dose of a drug.

LSD A powerful hallucinogen. Usually it comes in liquid form which is dropped on to blotting paper or sugar cubes, for example, and swallowed or dissolved on the tongue. It changes a person's senses and perspective but the impact may depend on their mood. Users may experience frightening 'trips' and occasionally flashbacks after taking the drug. Also called acid, tabs, trips.

magic mushrooms mushrooms that contain a chemical that gives a hallucinogenic effect. The main

danger comes from how the user acts after taking the drug. The user also has to be careful that they are taking the correct mushroom - certain mushrooms can be lethal.

overdose When too much of a drug is taken, leading to physical or mental illness or even death.

paranoia When someone suspects or distrusts others, without justification.

poppers The street name for amyl nitrite, a legal liquid that is sold in shops. Sniffing poppers gives a quick rush of blood to the brain. They can cause dizziness, nausea, fainting and stroke-like symptons and may damage the immune system.

propaganda Information that actively promotes ideas or beliefs.

prostitution Having sex for money.

psychiatrist A doctor who treats mental illness.

psychosis A severe breakdown of the mind, often leading to delusions.

punter A slang term for a customer, or sometimes for a prostitute's client.

rattling A slang term for the feeling a drug addict has when they need drugs.

rehab Short for rehabilitation. A rehab centre tries to help people to stop using drugs. Also see page 41.

schizophrenia A disorder that causes severe disruption to a person's mind, often causing delusions.

speed A type of amphetamine.

stimulant A type of drug that increases energy or concentration.

stoned A slang term for when someone has taken drugs and is not completely in touch with reality.

wrack off A slang term, meaning to play truant.

47

Index

Getting active!

On your own:
Put together a plan for a website that will make young people think about drugs issues. What will you include? How will you make your information accessible? Will you aim parts of the site at different age groups?

In pairs:
Research the law on drugs. Which drugs fall into each category? What are the penalties for using and supplying these drugs? Try to find out what people think about these laws - either by using the media or by using a questionnaire. Think of at least five questions to ask - for example - should cannabis be a legal drug?

In groups:
Organise a debate on a drug-related topic of your choice, for example, 'Cannabis taking leads to the use of hard drugs' or 'People should be able to choose to take drugs if they wish' etc. Organise people to take both sides of the argument and conclude with an audience vote on the issue. Some people could use a profile of one of the interviewees in this book.